W9-DFU-837

DISCARD

TWEEN 371.33 W

DIGITAL AND INFORMATION LITERACY ™

CREATING ELECTRONIC GRAPHIC ORGANIZERS

PHILIP WOLNY

rosen publishing's
rosen
central®

New York

Published in 2011 by The Rosen Publishing Group, Inc.
29 East 21st Street, New York, NY 10010

Copyright © 2011 by The Rosen Publishing Group, Inc.

First Edition

Library of Congress Cataloging-in-Publication Data

Wolny, Philip.
Creating electronic graphic organizers / Philip Wolny. — 1st ed.
    p. cm. — (Digital and information literacy)
Includes bibliographical references and index.
ISBN 978-1-4358-9428-0 (library binding)
ISBN 978-1-4488-0596-9 (pbk)
ISBN 978-1-4488-0603-4 (6-pack)
1. Information visualization — Juvenile literature. 2. Graphic organizers — Juvenile literature. 3. System analysis — Data processing — Juvenile literature. I. Title.
QA76.9.I52W65 2011
371.33–dc22

                                                          2010002501

Manufactured in the United States of America

CPSIA Compliance Information: Batch #S10YA: For further information, contact Rosen Publishing, New York, New York, at 1-800-237-9932.

CONTENTS

INTRODUCTION

What's the best way to solve a problem or make a decision? How about making a plan, or putting forth a pro/con argument? At times, this is an easy process, especially if the problem or decision is a relatively simple one. Often, however, just thinking something through is not enough to arrive at a satisfactory conclusion or plan of action. In these more difficult and complicated cases, a good plan of attack is to visualize the problem.

There are many ways that we visualize things in our lives to make them simpler and easier to deal with. For example, if we have a long list of chores to complete, we might list them, study the list, and then arrange them in order of importance. Creating a visual list of the work that needs to be done allows us to figure out which jobs are the most pressing and thus need to be done sooner, rather than later. When we are driving to an unfamiliar place, we often consult a map, whether a traditional foldout type or one generated by the Internet. This is because it's easier to find our way if we visualize the route, rather than get verbal directions from someone.

You can apply similar visual or graphic strategies to almost any project or task. When we organize information graphically, the visual formats we use for containing and presenting the data are known as graphic organizers. Some of the most common forms of graphic organizers are those we

see every day: maps, timelines, flowcharts, calendars, and various kinds of charts and graphs, like pie charts and bar graphs. These visual tools help people better understand complicated pieces of information and how they relate to each other. They can also help people examine and analyze problems, discover solutions, and arrive at logical conclusions.

Graphic organizers can help us make better sense of information we have already obtained or learned. Writing a book report for school, for instance, can be easier if you start by jotting down a rough plot outline (a type of graphic organizer) on a piece of paper. Or you can compose a character chart, with a column for names, physical and personality traits, important actions, memorable or revealing quotes, and relationship to the protagonist.

Graphic organizers can also visually demonstrate a process or the sequence and flow of a set of events. A calendar, for example, is a type of graphic organizer. It allows one to visualize a set of days and how one's time must be organized during those days in order to accommodate the various penciled-in tasks, appointments, and deadlines. A timeline of American history is a chronological list of dates and the important events that occurred on them. By following this stream of crucial moments from the past to the present, the timeline teaches us the sweeping story of our nation in a very efficient manner.

When we need to compare and contrast two or more things, graphic organizers are the tools to use. For example, if we are having a debate about a controversial topic, we can make a diagram that lists the arguments for and against the issue. In science class, we may need to sort through the many similarities and differences among the various great apes. Graphic organizers can help us identify and visually indicate the traits all the members of this family share and the distinctions that set orangutans, gorillas, chimpanzees, and humans apart.

Those wishing to create graphic organizers were once restricted to paper and pen. Now, thanks to the widespread availability and use of personal computers and the Internet, it is the era of electronic graphic organizers. Graphic organizers that once had to be constructed, drawn, and inked by hand or photocopied from workbooks are now just a few mouse clicks away on our computer screens.

Chapter 1

Why Are Electronic Graphic Organizers Useful?

To an extent never before possible or even imagined, information is all around us. It streams past us via television, radio, computers, and even our cell phones, twenty-four hours a day, seven days a week. For much of the twentieth century, the information we gained about the world came mainly from printed materials (books, magazines, and newspapers), as well as television and radio. With the growth of the Internet in the 1990s, there is more information available at our fingertips than ever before.

Presenting Information Visually

Much of the information in print, broadcast, and online media is presented visually. This is true whether we are gathering information for school, work, or pleasure. Open any newspaper or textbook. A history book may feature timelines showing important historical events. A newspaper article on

Timeline

12,000–4000 BCE	Ancestors of the Alaskan Indians, Inuits, Aleuts, and Inupiaqs travel to Alaska from Asia over a land bridge.
1728	Vitus Bering sails through the Bering Strait and along the Alaskan coastline.
1741	Bering sails into the Gulf of Alaska and lands on Kayak Island, becoming the first European in Alaska.
1778	British explorer Captain James Cook travels and maps the Alaskan coast.
1784	Russians build a settlement at Three Saints Bay on Kodiak Island.
1799	The Russian-American Company is given control of Alaska.
1867	Russia sells Alaska to the United States for $7.2 million.
1880	Gold is found near present-day Juneau.
1898	Gold is found in Nome, sparking the Klondike Gold Rush.
1900	Juneau becomes Alaska's capital.
1912	Alaska becomes a U.S. territory.
1914	The first railroad is built in Alaska.
1942	During World War II, the Japanese occupy the islands of Attu and Kiska; residents of the Aleutian Islands are evacuated to other parts of Alaska until the war ends in 1945.
1943	The Alaska Highway is completed, connecting Alaska to Canada.
1955	Alaska drafts a constitution.
1957	Oil is discovered in the Kenai Peninsula.
1959	Alaska becomes the forty-ninth state.
1964	A powerful earthquake strikes Anchorage and the surrounding areas.
1968	Large oil deposits are discovered in Prudhoe Bay on the North Slope.
1971	The Alaska Native Claims Settlement Act is passed.
1977	The Trans-Alaska Pipeline is completed.

A timeline is a form of graphic organizer that not only tells you the order in which events occurred, but also helps you see how events relate to and influence each other.

American food habits may include a pie chart showing what percentage of our diets is made up of fats, carbohydrates, and proteins. A film or music magazine may include a bar graph showing the five highest-earning movies or albums for the year, with each bar representing an individual film's or album's sales.

Imagine that your parents buy something that needs assembly, like a piece of furniture. The instructions often include pictures showing numbered steps on how to put it together. This, too, is a graphic organizer. It presents crucial information—in this case, assembly instructions—in a visual format that better demonstrates how to successfully complete a task than words alone would.

There are hundreds of different kinds of graphic organizers. In this book, however, we will be concentrating on ones that are commonly used for educational purposes. It is likely that you have already seen some of them and perhaps even created and used some yourself.

The Benefits of Graphic Organizers

What is it about graphic organizers that makes them so useful, especially in education? After all, why not simply use words to explore your subject and make your point in an argument or project? For one thing, the visual presentation of information has been shown to improve learning for many students. Some students actually absorb information better when using visual aids.

Many people are visual thinkers and visual learners. They think through things better when they use images to represent a problem or situation. For many such students, acquiring knowledge textually (the written word) or even verbally (the spoken word) can sometimes be difficult.

Better Recall, Greater Clarity

One reason why graphic organizers are so useful is that they can help with recall (memory). If the old saying is true, that a picture is worth a thousand

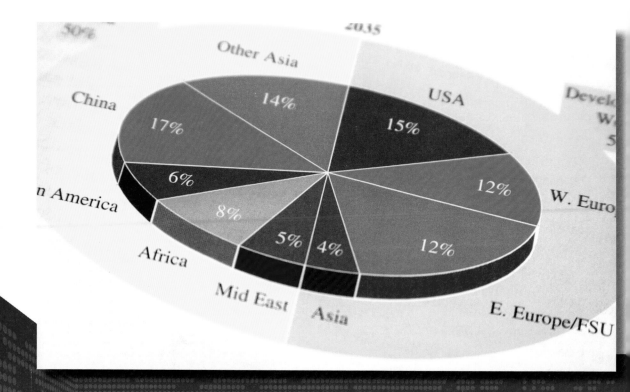

A pie chart is a great example of a simple graphic organizer that helps people easily visualize how parts or percentages relate to a greater whole.

words, a graphic organizer can help save lots of storage space in the brain. While results vary, some studies have shown that visualization tools and techniques improve learning and memory results.

Graphic organizers also improve the clarity of the information that is being presented. For example, imagine that you are given a twenty-page journal article. It is filled with long, dense paragraphs presenting the findings of a study that compares the health histories of hundreds of children who ate well-balanced meals with those of hundreds of children who ate only fast food. This would be a lot of information to take in all at once. Even if you read the whole article, you may not be able to see how all the diet, lifestyle, and environmental factors studied link up to create certain health trends. But

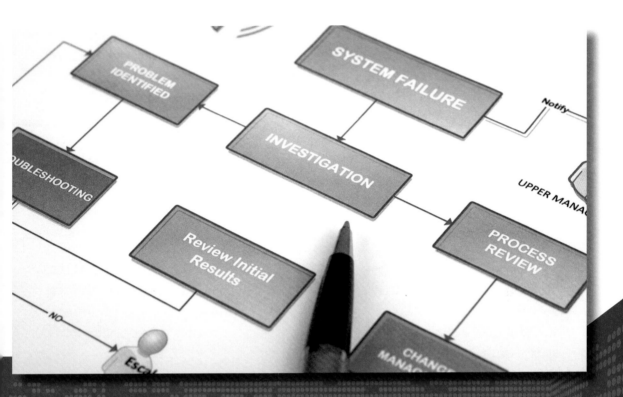

A good graphic organizer, like this flowchart, can guide its reader through the necessary steps to analyze and solve a problem or complete a series of tasks within a process.

if you are instead given a large chart that presents you with the same data, the information would be much easier to digest, the trends easier to spot, and the conclusions far easier to draw.

Flexibility

Graphic organizers are also useful because they are flexible. Each type of graphic organizer (pie chart, bar graph, flowchart, timeline) can be very simple in both design and content, or it can expand and become very complex and detailed (though still visually clear). The information presented can be basic or highly sophisticated.

In addition, the many forms that graphic organizers can take and the types of data they can convey increase their flexibility as information tools and learning aids. They can be used in the earliest brainstorming sessions for an upcoming essay. And they can be used in the final stages when you are mapping your paper paragraph-by-paragraph or creating a graph to include in the essay on your findings.

There are special graphic organizers for when you are brainstorming ideas. Other organizers, like concept maps, can be used to show how the ideas that are brainstormed may relate to each other. This allows you to find connections among what would otherwise seem like scattered thoughts. Once these connections are found, you can start building an argument or thesis for an essay and organizing your main points, perhaps using another graphic organizer, like an ice cream cone or describing wheel (see chapter 2). Concept maps can also be used to identify the main points of a chapter in a textbook or novel. This can make studying for exams or preparing book reports easier.

Critical Thinking

With the help of graphic organizers, students can think about and understand information in new ways. If a student's report relies only on text (words) to convey information, the tendency may be to simply copy or closely paraphrase text from his or her sources without really trying to understand what the authors are trying to say. Whatever learning is achieved in this kind of research and writing process is likely to be superficial (not very deep or comprehensive).

By presenting information visually, graphic organizers force your mind to absorb that information actively, rather than passively. They force you to figure out how the organizer is structured, what information it contains, and what that information shows. An author is not drawing conclusions for you. You have to draw them yourself based on the visual evidence before you. Rather than copying or memorizing material, you are absorbing it by interacting with it. This helps improve your critical thinking, which may be the most important skill of all in both learning and life.

MYTHS&FACTS

MYTH Electronic graphic organizers are only for people with design or technical skills.

FACT Graphic organizers can be used by everyone, from grade school learners to corporate executives.

MYTH Electronic graphic organizer programs are expensive.

FACT While some software is for purchase only, many graphic organizer programs are available free online (see chapter 3).

MYTH Graphic organizers are unfamiliar and intimidating tools.

FACT We already use many items in our daily lives that can be considered graphic organizers—calendars, report cards, computers' desktops, seating plans in school, etc. You've been using them your whole life! You're already familiar with them, and now you can use them to make your schoolwork easier, better, and much more fun!

Chapter 2

Getting Organized . . . and Electronic!

he Digital Information Age is a golden era for graphic organizers. Programs that help create electronic graphic organizers can be purchased as software or acquired for free online. They are light-years ahead of the old paper-based versions.

Starting Simple

Some of the simplest electronic graphic organizers are easily available online, often as a free download. There are other graphic organizers (both simple and more complex) that can be generated or used with readily available office software, such as Microsoft Excel and PowerPoint.

One of the most basic types of organizer is one you have surely seen before: the timeline. Sometimes, simply sitting down to organize events in the order in which they happened helps you grasp a subject or activity better. If you were asked to write a short paper about a field trip, for example, a timeline could help you organize your thoughts and begin to identify the key events and their sequence. In addition, timelines can be important and helpful elements in their own right for inclusion in a written report or multimedia presentation.

One online tool that helps you create timelines is available through TimeGlider (http://timeglider.com). If you are looking for a practice exercise to get yourself oriented, make a timeline using a TimeGlider template that shows some of the key events leading up to the American Revolution. Or you can simply create a practice timeline by listing all the major events of the past weekend, with day, date, and perhaps time of day listed, along with a brief description of each activity.

A Piece of the Pie

Another simple electronic graphic organizer is the pie chart. Each slice of a pie chart represents a different percentage, or piece, of the whole (100 percent). If you took a class survey on ice cream flavor preferences, for example, you could make a simple spreadsheet in a program like Excel. Each row would be devoted to an ice cream flavor (vanilla, chocolate, strawberry), and each column would show the number of students (and the resulting percentage) who prefer that specific flavor of ice cream.

If you then clicked on the Excel spreadsheet's automatic chart generating function, you would end up with a pie chart showing the whole class's ice cream preferences. Each piece of the pie would represent the percentage of students in the class who preferred a certain ice cream flavor. The biggest piece would represent the most popular flavor.

Speaking of Pies and Ice Cream . . .

Another pie-shaped data organizer that is useful is the describing wheel, another simple type of graphic organizer. The template is a basic wheel with a circle at the center containing the name of the thing described. You place your various descriptions along the spaces formed by the "spokes" of the

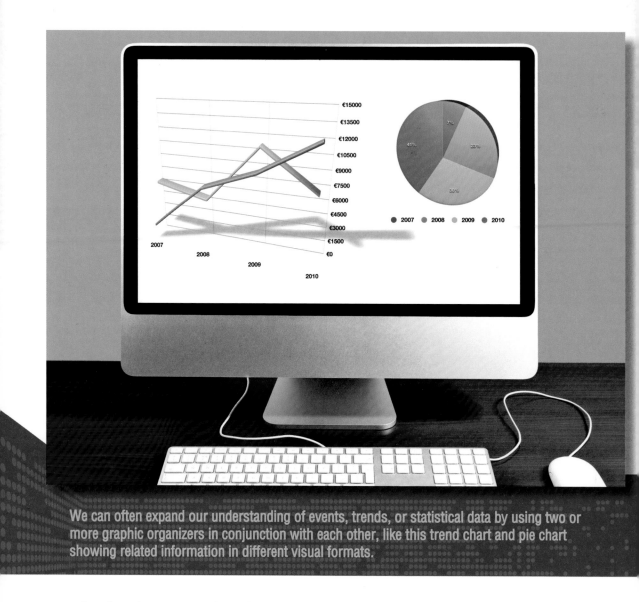

We can often expand our understanding of events, trends, or statistical data by using two or more graphic organizers in conjunction with each other, like this trend chart and pie chart showing related information in different visual formats.

wheel. A basic template for this kind of graphic organizer—and many others—can be downloaded in a portable document format (PDF) from Education Place (http://www.eduplace.com). In addition, by using PowerPoint or any similar graphics program, you can easily create an unlimited number of these kinds of wheel graphs, specially tailored to your needs.

BETTER HEALTH THROUGH ICE CREAM CONES!

Better Health Through Ice Cream Cones!

Let's say you have been asked to write a five-paragraph essay on the topic of achieving good health. You might use either the describing wheel or the ice cream cone to flesh out the main components of good health: exercise, balanced diet, regular checkups, stress reduction, and a support network of friends and family. Each of these components, in turn, would be discussed in one of your essay's five paragraphs. Just like that, your essay is practically written already!

A graphic organizer known as the ice cream cone is similar to the describing wheel. The label of the general idea or topic is written on the cone part of the diagram, and in each scoop of ice cream are placed your various descriptions or details relating to that topic. While the wheel design may list elements that are all equal in value or importance, the cone design gives you the option of ranking descriptive details by importance: The top scoop might be the most important, for instance. Both types of graphic organizers are good for brainstorming.

The Idea Rake

The idea rake—shaped somewhat like the garden tool used to collect leaves—is another graphic organizer designed to help you elaborate, or expand, on a topic. The "big" topic is listed at the top, while three subtopics are listed in the remaining spaces. There is also room below each rake tine to write in greater detail about each subtopic. The Education Place offers a basic idea rake template for download.

The Five W's

Another graphic organizer you can use in many different settings is the five W's chart. It is so named because the chart requires that you answer and fill in details relating to five questions: who, what, where, when, and why. The five W's chart can be organized into columns, or be designed like a star, oval, flower, or other figure. The design is less important than the organizer's intent: to get you to think about and understand more fully the events that you experience, read about, or plan to write about.

Several different types of five W's charts (and other types of graphic organizers) can be found at Enchanted Learning (http://www.enchantedlearning.com). For practice, use one of these charts to answer the five questions about the first American moon landing or the best day you had during your most recent summer vacation.

The Venn Diagram

One of the oldest types of graphic organizers is the Venn diagram. Englishman John Venn, a philosopher and logician, introduced the Venn diagram in 1880. It uses overlapping circles to compare and contrast two or more different things. By showing where the circles overlap,

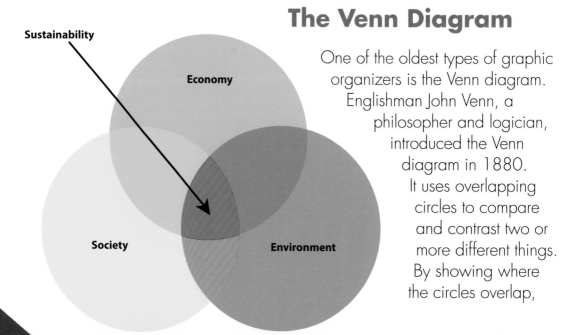

Sustainability

Economy

Society

Environment

The person who created this Venn diagram is visually conveying the idea that sustainable industries depend on the positive interaction of the economy, society, and the environment.

the graphic emphasizes what qualities the compared objects have in common. The parts of the circles that don't overlap are those qualities that are not shared by the two compared objects. Rather, these are the things unique to each.

KWL and KWHL Charts

A newer but highly useful type of graphic organizer is the KWL chart. Created by Donna Ogle in 1986, KWL is an organizer that can help you identify prior knowledge on a subject. It also helps track the knowledge that you gain in that subject while reading a book or conducting other kinds of research. In

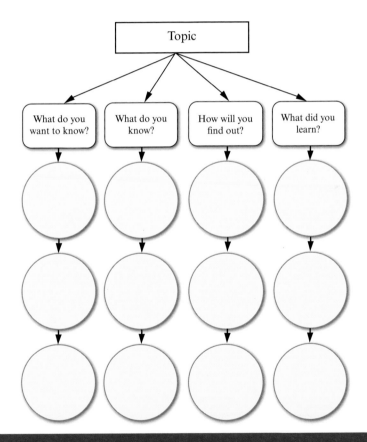

The KWHL chart pictured here allows users to track their information- and knowledge-gathering process as they explore a given topic.

this case, "K" stands for "what you know," "W" stands for "what you want to learn," and "L" stands for "what you have learned." Filling out each column as you go through the study of a subject lets you review your progress and literally chart how much you have learned and how much more you have to learn.

Another version of this kind of organizer is the KWHL chart. It is almost the same as the KWL chart, except that the additional "H" stands for "how." In other words, how will you obtain the knowledge? What resources, Web sites, formulas, techniques, or texts will you use to obtain it? The KWHL chart not only maps your progress, but it also lets you plan exactly how you will pursue your studies and what tools and resources you will use to reach your learning goals.

ISP Charts

"ISP" stands for "information, source, and page." These are the three key elements in this type of chart designed for use with research projects. Each element has its own column. The first (information) is for information, data, or quotes you find in your sources that may be useful to your research project. The second (source) is for the book or article where you found the information cited in the first column. And the third (page) is for the specific page number of the source where that information can be found.

This kind of chart is highly useful when identifying the facts, statistics, and quotations you wish to use in a report to help illustrate and support your argument and when citing this information in your footnotes and bibliography. An ISP chart also gives you a good visual overview of what sources you are using, what important types of sources may be missing from your research (not enough news periodicals or book-length works, for example, or perhaps too many Web sources), and what types of sources you still need to round out your research.

Concept Maps

One of the most common graphic organizers is the concept map, which shows the relationships among words, images, or ideas. Its elements are

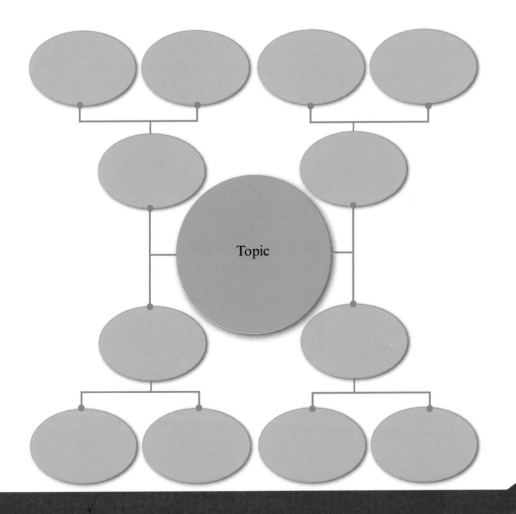

This is a typical concept map. It is broken down into four different subtopics, each of which is further broken down into items, concepts, or explanations.

connected by arrows that literally point out the relationships and interconnectedness of the various ideas or concepts. Concept maps can help you brainstorm, communicate complex ideas, and learn by bringing together old and new knowledge. They can also help you understand a concept, or at least help you identify what you don't understand about something.

Most important, concept maps help you discover how seemingly discon-nected ideas, subjects, or elements relate to each other. They let you uncover previously unrecognized connections. This can be a great help when trying to puzzle out a solution to a problem or fleshing out an essay that must make connections among various historical events, literary themes, or scientific processes, for example.

Cause and Effect: Fishbone Diagrams

A fishbone diagram goes by several names. It is also known as an Ishikawa diagram or a cause-and-effect diagram. While reading a novel for English class, for instance, we can use a fishbone diagram to map out how a character's actions affect the plot. In chemistry, we can use fishbone diagrams to record in detail the reactions that occur when various chemical solutions are mixed.

Let's take an example using Microsoft's Visio program, a popular soft-ware tool for creating diagrams. Imagine we are working on a fishbone diagram tracing the root causes of America's entry into World War II.

After opening the Visio program, select BUSINESS PROCESS from the CHOOSE DRAWING TYPE window. This opens a ready-made template for a cause-and-effect diagram. The diagram consists of the spine (a horizontal line that represents your subject or main effect, in this case U.S. involvement in WWII) and the shorter diagonal lines radiating from the spine (the causes of U.S. involvement in WWII). Clicking on the spine allows you to name the diagram. You then decide on how many categories or causes to include.

For example, some of your categories or main causes could be German territorial aggression, the Blitz of London, atrocities committed against Jewish and other civilian populations in Europe, and Japan's bomb-ing of Pearl Harbor. Feeding into each of these, in turn, you may have secondary causes of the main causes (for example, the Treaty of Versailles that ended WWI left Germany so impoverished and humiliated that a mili-tant nationalism soon took hold and led to bitter aggression and militarism). These secondary causes can be added to the main categories or causes

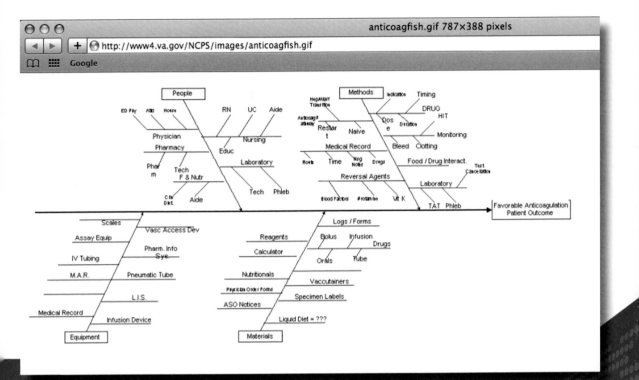

This fishbone diagram from the U.S. Department of Veterans Affairs (http://www4.va.gov) shows how four distinct treatment elements (essentially causes of good health)—People, Methods, Equipment, and Materials—affect a patient who has blood coagulation problems.

by dragging and dropping them in place. They will branch off of your main causes as smaller "fishbones" attached to the main "fishbones."

When labeling the diagram spine and various sets of fishbones, you can click on any of the diagram's elements—its spine and various sets of main and secondary fishbones—and type in the labels and descriptive information you desire. For some examples of cause-and-effect diagrams, go to Enchanted Learning's graphic organizers section and click on CAUSE AND EFFECT.

Chapter 3

Finding Good Electronic Graphic Organizers Online

So far, we have touched upon some common graphic organizers. In this chapter, we will look at some online resources and software, both free and for purchase. Some products offer ready-made templates of graphic organizers you can use immediately. Other programs allow you to edit these templates or create your own. We will continue to examine new examples of graphic organizers as we explore some of the tools available.

MindMapper

A software program like MindMapper takes the basic idea of mind maps (concept maps) and transforms it into a flexible and convenient digital tool. One especially useful aspect of software like this is the ready-made templates it provides. You can begin making a mind map right after opening

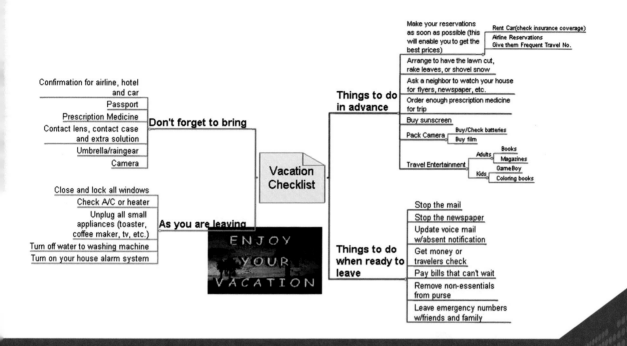

Pictured here is an example of a mind map that can easily be created using a Web-based electronic graphic organizer. This one, which was used to plan a vacation, was created with MindMapper software (http://www.mindmapper.com).

the program. You can choose from brainstorming templates, fishbone (cause and effect) diagrams, or a variety of other concept maps.

Once you have started a mind map, you will soon recognize the benefits of using software to create a graphic organizer instead of the traditional pen-and-ink (and eraser) approach. You can move idea clusters simply by pointing and clicking and easily edit text anywhere on your map. Rather than consuming lots of time (and art supplies) to design, draw, and revise a printed graphic organizer, MindMapper lets you choose quickly and easily from hundreds of different colors, fonts, and designs. You can even change your mind and rework the organizer's entire appearance in just a few mouse clicks. And if you like the look of handmade graphic organizers and worry that electronic ones will look too cold or lack personality, fear not! Different styles of digital "drawing"—even ones that look hand-drawn—are available. To learn more about MindMapper, visit the site (http://www.mindmapper.com).

Inspiration

MindMapper can be used by students for schoolwork, but the software was designed mainly for business applications. Other programs are designed specifically for students, however. One such program is called Inspiration, and it is designed for users between six and twelve years old. One of the big advantages of Inspiration is that it has more than 120 different templates. The types of graphic organizers included in the program include those designed for planning and brainstorming, science, social studies, and language arts, among others.

Inspiration's visual interface (the way it appears on-screen to the user) offers a simple and user-friendly set of tools right at your fingertips. As with some other office software, the toolbars on top and graphic icon palettes to the left let you select tools quickly and easily. For a mind or concept map, for example, you can construct diagrams, starting with a main idea, simply by hitting ENTER—each new idea appears in a new symbol, or box. You can then add ideas that are connected to the main concept with lines or arrows.

For a short video introduction to Inspiration and examples of how its graphic organizers work, visit the company's product demo (http://www. Inspiration.com).

MindGenius Mind Mapping Software

One of the many things that makes the MindGenius Mind Mapping Software useful is its mapping functions, which help students plan out their essays. Users have the ability to change the graphic organizer's structure and content at any time with just a few mouse clicks. This means that revisions are far easier and cleaner than they would be compared to writing out an outline on paper that has numerous erasures, cross-outs, arrows, and other visually confusing and sloppy edits.

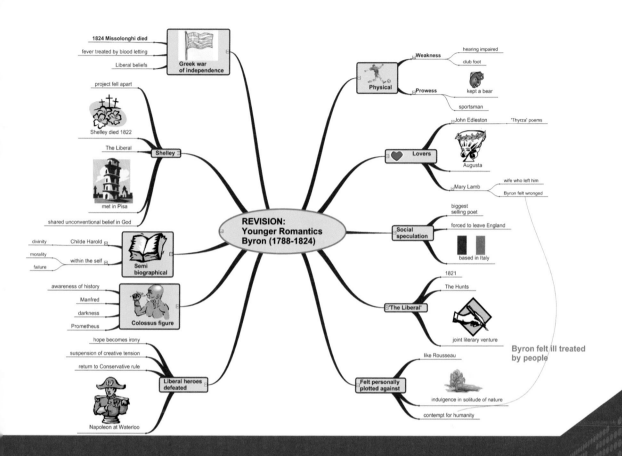

In this concept map created with MindGenius Mind Mapping Software (http://www.mindgenius.com), the user has broken down the main topic—the life and work of the Romantic poet Lord Byron—into various subtopics and themes.

Another convenient feature of MindGenius Mind Mapping Software (http://www.mindgenius.com) is how easy it is to convert a mind map into various documents in Microsoft Office, most notably Word. This allows you to import your Mind Map outline into Word and "build it out" into prose, converting each line item of the outline into a text paragraph, using the main points contained in the outline to flesh out your argument. Programs like MindGenius make it a fairly easy process to go from the idea stage to the outline to a well-organized and content-rich essay.

Freeware: The Price Is Right

Unfortunately, software can be expensive. If you cannot afford to buy graphic organizer software for your home computer, check with your school or public librarian or computer lab teacher to see if any of these programs are available for use on public computers. Even without expensive software, you can create good electronic graphic organizers with the help of free downloads from reputable educational Web sites.

One of these free online sources is FreeMind (http://freemind. sourceforge.net/wiki/index.php/Main_Page), available for a variety of computer operating systems. Like much "freeware," it gets the job done, but the results may not look as professional or advanced as those produced by computer programs you pay for. As Tim Haddock says in his review for *Macworld*, "FreeMind is not going to win any beauty contests."

A particularly useful feature of FreeMind is the ability it gives you to use images (such as saved photos) in place of text nodes. Using this feature, you could create a map of the U.S. president's cabinet, for example, using cabinet members' portraits to identify their departments, along with their names and official positions. FreeMind even lets you import mind maps made with other mind mapping software.

With the aim of researching the many potential uses of graphic organizers, Tufts University, in Medford, Massachusetts, has set up a Web site that lets users discuss, present, and create organizers using its free software. It is called the Visual Understanding Environment (VUE), and can be downloaded at its site (http://vue.tufts.edu). The Tufts site also has a wealth of other resources involving electronic graphic organizers.

Some other sources of electronic graphic organizers that can be downloaded for free include XMind (www.xmind.net), Freeology (http://freeology.com/graphicorgs), Education Place (www.eduplace.com/graphicorganizer), edHelper (http://edhelper.com/teachers/graphic_organizers.htm), NetRover (www.netrover.com/~kingskid/graphic/graphic.htm),BusyTeachersCafe (www.busyteacherscafe.com/printables/graphicorganizers.htm), Education Oasis (www.educationoasis.com/

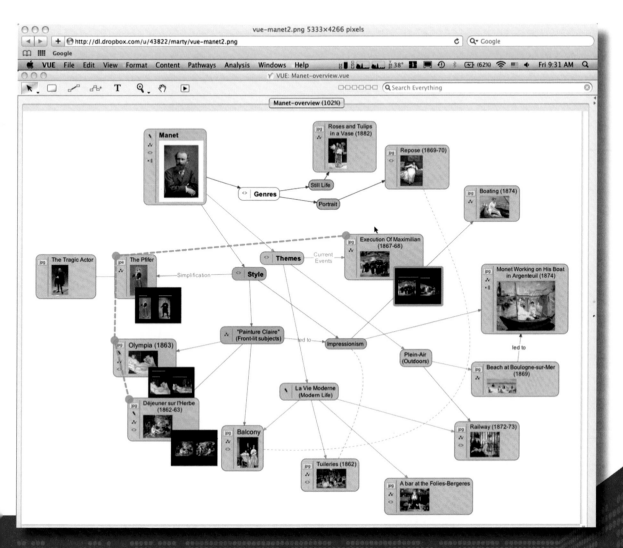

Visually appealing graphic organizers often mix text and images. Here, you can see how works by the artist Manet interconnect. This concept map is on Tuft University's VUE Project Web site (http://vue.tufts.edu).

curriculum/graphic_organizers.htm), Microsoft Office (http://office.microsoft.com/en-us/templates/CT102819181033.aspx), Teachnology (www.teach-nology.com/worksheets/graphic), and Holt Interactive (http://my.hrw.com/nsmedia/intgos/html/igo.htm).

File   Edit   View   Favorites   Tools   Help

BEWARE MALWARE!

Beware Malware!

When downloading free software or graphic organizer PDFs, be very careful that you are not also downloading malicious software, or malware. Malware is a large category of malicious software that users unknowingly import to their computers when they download other software. The malware hides within and piggybacks on this legitimate software. Once inside your computer, it may attack your hardrive, seize control of the computer, send e-mails from your account, or steal data. It may tamper with your computer, its hardrive, software, personal information, and e-mail address book. Do research on any Web site you plan to use for free software and make sure no one has filed any complaints about the site or claims that it has unleashed malware within his or her computer. Ask librarians and computer lab teachers for a list of reputable free software providers, and never download something to a school or library computer without permission. Also make sure your computer is protected by antivirus software!

Be careful when downloading graphic organizers that seem to be free. Some are copyright protected, so read all the fine print. In addition, some resources provide you with one or two sample downloads before they start charging, and others have locks or restrictions that prevent full use of the download. Check out Graphic.org (http://www.graphic.org/organizers/free-graphic-organizers.html) for a list of the best Web sites offering free downloads of graphic organizers with no strings attached.

TEN GREAT QUESTIONS
TO ASK A LIBRARIAN

1. What is the best graphic organizer that I can purchase to help me not only in school, but also in future educational and work environments?

2. What are good online resources where I can learn more about graphic organizers?

3. What are the different categories of graphic organizers, and what tasks are they best used for?

4. Where can I learn about the latest research on graphic organizers and why they are effective as learning aids?

5. Can I benefit from using graphic organizers, even if I'm not a visual learner?

6. Which is better: constructing graphic organizers yourself, or having a teacher print ones to fill out?

7. If I'm new at using graphic organizers, where is the best place to start?

8. What if I don't have a computer at home? Are there other places I can access, download, design, and print out graphic organizers? What are reputable sites for free downloads of graphic organizer programs or worksheets?

9. What are some examples of graphic organizers being used by teachers, school administrators, businesspeople, economists, military planners, and other professionals?

10. How do I know which graphic organizers are best suited to a particular problem or task?

Chapter 4

Visualizing Success!

So far, we have seen what types of charts, diagrams, and mind/concept maps are out there and have discussed some examples of their use. What are some other ways to use electronic graphic organizers in reports and projects? Whether you are doing an oral presentation and need visual aids, turning in a book report, trying to generate ideas for a school newspaper, or simply studying for an exam, graphic organizers are of invaluable assistance.

Integrating Graphic Organizers with Your Work

While many people save their graphic organizers as stand-alone (separate) files, they are great additions to other documents, such as PowerPoint presentations or essays written on a word processor. Often, integrating your graphic organizer into the body of your report is as simple as copying and pasting it into the text of a Word document or onto a presentation slide. If you

Charts and other graphic organizers can be used as project add-ons to clarify and summarize the information contained in a written or oral report in a visually compelling and easily readable way.

have generated a graphic organizer and do not expect to make any further changes to it, it can often be saved as a PDF or in a picture file (like a JPEG).

In some cases, a diagram you create in one program can be pasted into another and edited. For example, a Visio chart can be plugged into a Microsoft Word document. It appears as a normal image file in the document until you click on it, making it active for further edits. Often, however, it is recommended that you try to do as much revision as possible in the actual software used to create the file.

Striking a Balance

Electronic graphic organizers are great tools, but they are not the be-all, end-all of school assignments. They are great for inspiring new ways of thinking and guiding debate on a topic or task. You may often use them as a tool to initiate and organize ideas, rather than as a finished product. A fishbone diagram describing the actions of characters in Mark Twain's classic *The Adventures of Huckleberry Finn* and the effects of these actions on the plot might provide the basic bones of a book report, but it is the writing itself and your own interpretation that will give the essay flesh and blood.

Also, consider electronic graphic organizers as potential add-ons to your main body of work. For example, they can be used as elements within a larger whole, like a history essay that includes a timeline or a science lab report that includes a pie chart or bar graph. A group project on how state government works could potentially include several organizers—an organizational chart with the governor and other officials; a concept map showing how the branches of government work together; and perhaps even a pie chart showing the representation of women and minorities in state government.

Using Graphic Organizers in a Project, from Start to Finish

To put it all in perspective, let's envision a class project in which graphic organizers can be used in different ways and at different stages—from the sketching of basic ideas to the final presentation. Let's say the class is doing a project on local weather. They want to examine how well or poorly their town has responded to severe weather in the last fifty years. Perhaps they want to know if their local government has gotten better, worse, or stayed the same in it reaction to extreme weather.

The first step is to brainstorm some common forms of extreme weather. These could include heavy rainfall and floods, blizzards, heat waves, cold snaps, droughts, tornadoes, and hurricanes. Useful graphic organizers for

Graphic organizers are a great tool for collaborative work. Here, group members brainstorm while one group member does on-the-spot Internet research using a laptop and wireless connection.

this stage of the process might be the describing wheel or ice cream cone diagrams.

If it is a large enough group, they can split into smaller groups. While some of the subgroups come up with severe weather patterns to include in the analysis, others might brainstorm different sources for research. As the group gets deeper into the research and begins collecting data and stories, a cause-and-effect diagram might come in handy. The group may discover that their town was once not so well-prepared for bad weather. But, over time, the town's emergency preparedness and response may have improved.

When crafting their fishbone diagrams, the group can discuss what actions and decisions caused improvements or failures in weather preparedness and response over time.

Group members can now begin drawing some information from their fishbone diagram and use it to start a rough draft of a timeline. As the group gathers information from different sources, it might even be a good idea to assign one person the task of managing the timeline. Seeing when certain events happened will let group members know where gaps in the record are. A timeline will also help tell the story of local extreme weather in the last fifty years.

After a few weeks of intensive meetings, brainstorming, data gathering, and using graphic organizers to divide the work, it is time to present the research and conclusions. What are some of the graphic organizers the group might include in the final presentation?

The timeline could be a helpful visual aid for the project, both printed out and projected in a slideshow for the class. A cause-and-effect chart demonstrating some of the main conclusions about severe weather and the town's changing response to it could also be highly useful for the audience. A bar graph showing the amount of money the town has spent on weather-related disaster response over the years and a pie chart revealing what percentage of the town's budget is spent on weather response would be very interesting.

In addition, the group might print and hand out completed KWL or KWHL charts to students and teachers in the audience. These will walk the audience through the group's learning and research process during the development of the project. Another idea is to distribute blank KWL or KWHL charts to the audience and ask them to fill these out. This is a great way to determine if the group did a good job of getting its information and conclusions across.

An Electronic Future

Hopefully, using electronic graphic organizers will help you approach learning and doing homework and classwork in new and different ways. As you

A student uses an Apple iPad to check the latest news for a current events project. Electronic graphic organizers will become ever more prevalent and popular as students, workers, and other computer users engage with an increasingly visual and digital world of content.

become more familiar and comfortable with them, you will discover which ones work best for your purposes. Electronic graphic organizers are becoming more useful and popular in an increasingly dynamic and visual world. By mastering them and using them to expand your knowledge, organize your thoughts, increase your understanding of how things fit together, and clearly present vital information, electronic graphic organizers will serve you well throughout high school, college, and beyond, into the workplace of the future!

GLOSSARY

brainstorm To come up with solutions to a problem or generate ideas by thinking intensely about them and then writing down or discussing anything that comes to mind.

describing wheel A wheel-shaped graphic organizer in which the user fills in his or her ideas on a topic in the spokes of the wheel; the hub of the wheel is the topic.

fishbone diagram A graphic organizer that demonstrates cause-and-effect relationships; also known as an Ishikawa or cause-and-effect diagram.

five W's chart A chart that lists in descriptive detail the elements of a topic, event, narrative, or other subject being discussed or analyzed; the five W's are who, what, why, where, and when.

freeware Software that is distributed free of charge over the Internet.

ice cream cone A graphic organizer in which the scoops of the cone list descriptive details or major illustrative points, and the cone represents the topic or main idea.

idea rake A graphic organizer shaped like a rake. The handle of the rake is the topic or main idea; the tines of the rake are descriptive details or illustrative points that elaborate on the main idea.

ISP chart A graphic organizer that, in three distinct columns, lists the information the user has gathered, its sources, and its page references.

JPEG A common form of photographic compression within an electronic file for using and sending images on computers and via the Internet. JPEG is an acronym for the Joint Photographic Experts Group, the committee that created the image coding standards for JPEGs.

KWL diagram A diagram that lets people list what they already know about a subject at the beginning of a course of study, what they want to know by the end, and what they have in fact learned at the end of the process.

mind map A diagram that represents words, ideas, tasks, or other elements that are connected to each other and all derive in turn from a central concept or idea.

PDF This stands for portable document format, a file format created by Adobe Systems for easy and efficient electronic document exchange.

pie chart A circular chart that is divided into sections representing numerical percentages of a whole.

timeline A graphic representation of the chronological and linear unfolding of historical events.

tree chart A graphic organizer in which ideas, descriptive details, or illustrative points are listed on a tree's branches. The tree's trunk is the topic or main idea.

visualization The process of forming a mental image of something, typically something immaterial or intangible, like a concept or idea.

FOR MORE INFORMATION

Computers for Youth
322 Eighth Avenue, Floor 12A
New York, NY 10001
(212) 563-7300
Web site: http://www.cfy.org
Computers for Youth provides inner-city students with home computers and
    provides training, technical support, and online education so that stu-
    dents can perform better in school.

Educational Computing Organization of Ontario (ECOO)
10 Morrow Avenue, Suite 202
Toronto, ON M6R 2J1
Canada
(416) 489-1713
Web site: http://www.ecoo.org
The ECOO helps teachers and students integrate computer learning into the
    educational process.

GetNetWise
Internet Education Foundation
1634 I Street NW
Washington DC 20009
Web site: http://www.getnetwise.org
GetNetWise is part of the Internet Education Foundation, which works to
    provide a safe online environment for children and families.

International Technology Education Association (ITEA)
1914 Association Drive, Suite 201
Reston, VA 20191-1539

(703) 860-2100
Web site: http://www.iteaconnect.org
The ITEA promotes technology education and literacy.

Internet Education Foundation
1634 I Street NW, Suite 1100
Washington, DC, 20006
(202) 637-0968
Web site: http://neted.org
The Internet Education Foundation is a nonprofit organization dedicated to
    informing the public about Internet education.

Ontario Institute for Studies in Education
University of Toronto
252 Bloor Street West
Toronto, ON M5S 1V6
Canada
(416) 978-2011
Web site: http://www.oise.utoronto.ca/oise
The Ontario Institute for Studies in Education is one of Canada's most impor-
    tant centers for the study of education.

Public Broadcasting Service
Teacher Resources
2100 Crystal Drive
Arlington, VA 22202
Web site: http://www.pbs.org/teachers
The Public Broadcasting Service offers various resources for teachers and
    students, including a wealth of lesson plans using graphic organizers.

School of Education
University of California, Davis
One Shields Avenue
Davis, CA 95616
(530) 752-5887
Web site: http://education.ucdavis.edu
The School of Education at UC Davis promotes the use of graphic organizers in classroom instruction. The future teachers that the school trains learn the benefits of using graphic organizers as teaching and learning aids and recognize graphic organizers as fun and involving tools for entering more deeply into all subject areas.

Web Sites

Due to the changing nature of Internet links, Rosen Publishing has developed an online list of Web sites related to the subject of this book. This site is updated regularly. Please use this link to access this list:

http://www.rosenlinks.com/dil/cego

FOR FURTHER READING

Appleman, Dan. *Always Use Protection: A Teen's Guide to Safe Computing.* New York, NY: Apress, 2004.

Bailey, Diane. *Cyber Ethics.* New York, NY: Rosen Publishing, 2008.

Cobb, Allan B. *Looking at the Interdependence of Plants, Animals, and the Environment with Graphic Organizers* (Using Graphic Organizers to Study the Living Environment). New York, NY: Rosen Publishing, 2006.

Farnette, Cherrie, Marjorie Frank, Kathleen Bullock, and Cary Grayson. *Graphic Organizers for Writing.* Nashville, TN: Incentive Publications, 2006.

Frank, Marjorie, Jill Norris, and Kathleen Bullock. *Graphic Organizers for Math.* Nashville, TN: Incentive Publications, 2007.

Hawthorn, Kate. *A Young Person's Guide to the Internet.* New York, NY: Routledge, 2005.

Hock, Randolph. *The Extreme Searcher's Internet Handbook.*2nd ed. Medford, NJ: CyberAge Books, 2007.

Kramer, Jan. *Learning About Simple Machines with Graphic Organizers* (Graphic Organizers in Science). New York, NY: Rosen Publishing, 2009.

Kravetz, Jonathan. *Learning About Energy with Graphic Organizers* (Graphic Organizers in Science). New York, NY: PowerKids Press, 2006.

Parker, Christi E. *30 Graphic Organizers for Reading* (Graphic Organizers to Improve Literacy Skills). Huntington Beach, CA: Shell Education, 2006.

Parker, Christi E. *30 Graphic Organizers for Writing* (Graphic Organizers to Improve Literacy Skills). Huntington Beach, CA: Shell Education, 2007.

Reed, Jennifer. *Picture This!: Graphic Organizers.* Poulsbo, WA: Barker Creek Publishing, 2007.

Shaw, Maura D. *Mastering Online Research.* Cincinnati, OH: Writer's Digest Books, 2007.

Willard, Nancy. *Cyber-Safe Kids, Cyber-Savvy Teens.* New York, NY: Jossey-Bass, 2007.

BIBLIOGRAPHY

Burke, Jim. *Tools for Thought: Graphic Organizers for Your Classroom.* Chicago, IL: Heinemann, 2002.

Chang, Maria L. *Science Graphic Organizers & Mini-Lessons* (Best Practices in Action). Washington, DC: Teaching Resources, 2006.

Drapeau, Patti. *Differentiating with Graphic Organizers: Tools to Foster Critical and Creative Thinking.* Thousand Oaks, CA: Corwin Press, 2008.

Education Oasis. "Graphic Organizers." 2009. Retrieved September 2009 (http://www.educationoasis.com/curriculum/graphic_organizers.htm).

Education Place. "Graphic Organizers." Retrieved September 2009 (http://www.eduplace.com/graphicorganizer).

Education World. "Educator Software Review: Inspiration." March 27, 2002. Retrieved September 2009 (http://www.educationworld.com/a_tech/tech/tech124.shtml).

Eduscapes. "Teacher Tap: Time-Saving Starters." Retrieved September 2009 (http://eduscapes.com/tap/topic73.htm).

Enchanted Learning. "Graphic Organizers." Retrieved September 2009 (http://www.enchantedlearning.com/graphicorganizers).

Graphic.org. "The Graphic Organizer." Retrieved September 2009 (http://www.graphic.org).

Haddock, Tim. "Review: FreeMind 0.8.1: Java-Based Mind Mapping Freeware Favors Function Over Form." *Macworld*, November 2008. Retrieved September 2009 (http://www.macworld.com/article/136808/2008/11/freemind081.html).

McMackin, Mary. *Teaching Reading: Differentiated Instruction with Leveled Graphic Organizers: 40+ Reproducible, Leveled Organizers That Help You Teach Comprehension to ALL Learning Needs Easily and Effectively.* Washington, DC: Teaching Strategies, 2009.

Microsoft. "Show Historical Cause and Effect Using Visio." Retrieved December 2009 (http://office.microsoft.com/en-us/visio/HA010778461033.aspx).

Robb, Anina. *40 Graphic Organizers That Build Comprehension During Independent Reading.* Washington, DC: Teaching Resources, 2003.

Roberts, Jane. *25 Prewriting Graphic Organizers & Planning Sheets: Must-Have Tools to Help All Students Gather and Organize Their Thoughts to Jumpstart the Writing Process.* Washington, DC: Teaching Strategies, 2004.

Rock, B. "Three Types of Graphic Organizers to Use with Your Students." Associated Content, January 19, 2008. Retrieved September 2009 (http://www.associatedcontent.com/article/552309/three_types_of_graphic_organizers_to.html?cat=4).

Rutgers, the State University of New Jersey. "Rutgers Researcher Finds Visual Memory Is Better Than Previously Thought." *ScienceDaily*, July 26, 2001. Retrieved September 2009 (http://www.sciencedaily.com/releases/2001/07/010726103502.htm).

Scholastic. "Graphic Organizers for Reading Comprehension." 1996–2009. Retrieved September 2009 (http://www2.scholastic.com/browse/article.jsp?id=2983).

SuperKids Educational Software Review. "Inspiration Version 6." Retrieved September 2009 (http://www.superkids.com/aweb/pages/reviews/writing/1/inspirat/merge.shtml).

Technology Gear. "Graphic Organizer: A Valuable Tool to Show the Order and Comprehensiveness of the Students' Thought Process." October 12, 2008. Retrieved September 2009 (http://www.technologygear.net/graphic-organizer-a-valuable-tool-to-show-the-order-and-comprehensiveness-of-the-students-thought-process.html).

Tufts University. "Visual Understanding Environment (VUE)." Retrieved September 2009 (http://vue.tufts.edu).

INDEX

About the Author

Philip Wolny is an author and editor from New York whose previous jobs were made much easier by on-the-job education in the use of visual software, especially certain graphics software. His experience in the job market makes him a staunch proponent of learning about and utilizing these tools as early as possible.

Photo Credits

Cover (left), p. 1 (left) © www.istockphoto.com/Nicholas Moore; cover (second from left), p. 1 (second from left), p. 35 © www.istockphoto.com/René Mansi; cover (right), p. 1 (right), p. 29 © Courtesy of Visual Understanding Environment/University Academic Technology; cover (second from right), p. 1 (second from right) © www.istockphoto.com; cover (background), interior design © www.istockphoto.com; pp. 10, 11, 16 Shutterstock; p. 25 © SlimTech Systems, Inc. (www.mindmapper.com); p. 27 © MindGenius Mind Mapping Software; p. 33 © David Young-Wolff/Photo Edit; p. 37 © Kimberly White/Reuters/Landov.

Designer: Nicole Russo; Photo Researcher: Marty Levick